The Best
QUICK BREADS

The Best
QUICK BREADS

Muffins, Biscuits, Scones,
and Other Bread Basket Treats

By Gregg R. Gillespie

BLACK DOG
& LEVENTHAL
PUBLISHERS
NEW YORK

Published by
Black Dog & Leventhal Publishers, Inc.
151 West 19th Street
New York, NY 10011

Distributed by
Workman Publishing
708 Broadway
New York, NY 10003

Manufactured in Spain

ISBN 1-57912-295-7

Library of Congress Cataloging-in-Publication Data is on file and available
from Black Dog & Leventhal Publishers, Inc.

Cover and interior design by 27.12 Design, Ltd.
Interior layout by Cindy Joy
Photographs by Bill Melton, Wild Bill Studios

g f e d c b a

CONTENTS

APPLE-AND-PECAN MUFFINS

makes 12 to 14 muffins

2½ cups all-purpose flour
1 tsp. baking soda
1½ cups peeled, cored, and
 diced apple
½ cup chopped pecans
1 tsp. salt

1 large egg
1 cup buttermilk or sour milk
1½ cups packed light-brown
 sugar
¼ cup canola oil
1 tsp. vanilla extract

1. Position the rack in the center of the oven and preheat to 375 degrees. Lightly grease or line with paper baking cups fourteen 2¾-inch muffin cups.
2. In a large bowl, blend together the flour, baking soda, apples, pecans, and salt. In a medium bowl, beat the egg until foamy. Beat in the buttermilk, brown sugar, oil, and vanilla extract. Combine the two mixtures, blending until the dry ingredients are just moistened.
3. Spoon the batter into the prepared muffin cups, filling each about three-quarters full. Bake for 20 to 25 minutes, or until a cake tester or wooden toothpick inserted into the center of a muffin comes out clean. Cool in the pan on a wire rack for 5 to 7 minutes. Serve warm, or invert onto the rack to cool completely.

APRICOT-AND-WALNUT MUFFINS

makes 5 to 6 muffins

1⅔ cups all-purpose flour
2 tsp. baking powder
½ cup granulated sugar
¼ tsp. ground cinnamon
½ tsp. salt
1 large egg

¾ cup milk
⅓ cup butter or margarine, melted
½ cup apricot jam
½ cup chopped walnuts

1. Position the rack in the center of the oven and preheat to 400 degrees. Lightly grease or line with paper baking cups six (makes 5 to 6 muffins) 2¾-inch muffin cups.
2. In a large bowl, blend together the flour, baking powder, sugar, cinnamon, and salt. In a medium bowl, beat the egg until foamy. Beat in the milk and butter. Combine the two mixtures, blending until the dry ingredients are just moistened.
3. Spoon the batter into the prepared muffin cups, filling each about ¾ full. Lightly press 1 teaspoon of apricot jam into the center of each muffin. Sprinkle the top of each muffin with chopped walnuts. Bake for 20 to 25 minutes, or until a wooden toothpick inserted near the edge of a muffin (not into the jam filling) comes out clean. Cool in the pan on a wire rack for 5 to 7 minutes. Serve warm, or invert onto the rack to cool completely.

BANANA CROWNS

makes 11 to 12 muffins

2 cups all-purpose flour
¾ cup granulated sugar
1 tsp. baking soda
½ cup chopped walnuts
1 tsp. salt
2 large eggs

1½ cups (about 3 medium)
  mashed bananas
2 to 4 tbsp. mango jam
  or preserves
1 large banana,
  sliced into 24 pieces

1. Position the rack in the center of the oven and preheat to 375 degrees.
   Lightly grease or line with paper baking cups twelve 2¾-inch
   muffin cups.
2. In a large bowl, blend together the flour, sugar, baking soda, walnuts,
   and salt. In a small bowl, beat the eggs and mashed bananas until
   smooth. Combine the two mixtures, blending until the dry ingredients
   are just moistened.
3. Spoon the batter into the prepared muffin cups, filling each about
   ¾ full. Press ¼ teaspoon of the mango jam and a banana slice into
   the center of each cup. Bake for 15 to 20 minutes, or until a cake
   tester or wooden toothpick inserted near the edge of a muffin (not
   into the jam) comes out clean. Cool in the pan on a wire rack for 5 to
   7 minutes. Allow to cool to room temperature.

BLACKBERRY MUFFINS

makes 5 to 6 muffins

2½ cups all-purpose flour
1 tbsp. baking powder
½ tsp. salt
3 large eggs, separated
½ cup granulated sugar

¼ cup canola oil
⅔ cup milk
1 cup blackberries,
   rinsed and dried

1. Position the rack in the center of the oven and preheat to 400 degrees.
   Lightly grease or line with paper baking cups six 2¾-inch muffin cups.
2. In a large bowl, blend together the flour, baking powder, and salt.
   In a medium bowl, beat together the egg yolks, sugar, oil, and milk.
   In a small bowl, beat the egg whites until stiff but not dry. Fold the
   blackberries into the egg whites. Combine the dry ingredients and
   the egg yolk mixture, blending until just moistened. Gently fold in
   the egg whites.
3. Spoon the batter into the prepared muffin cups, filling each about
   ¾ full. Bake for 20 to 25 minutes, or until a cake tester or wooden
   toothpick inserted into the center of a muffin comes out clean.
   Cool in the pan on a wire rack for 5 to 7 minutes. Serve warm,
   or invert onto the rack to cool completely.

BLUEBERRY-BUTTERMILK MUFFINS

makes 5 to 6 muffins

2½ cups all-purpose flour
2½ tsp. baking powder
¼ tsp. salt
2 large eggs
1 cup granulated sugar

1 cup buttermilk or sour milk
¼ cup butter or margarine,
melted
1½ cups blueberries,
rinsed and dried

1. Position the rack in the center of the oven and preheat to 400 degrees.
   Lightly grease or line with paper baking cups six 2¾-inch muffin cups.
2. In a large bowl, blend together the flour, baking powder, and salt.
   In a medium bowl, beat the eggs until foamy. Beat in the sugar,
   buttermilk, and melted butter until smooth. Fold in the blueberries.
   Combine the two mixtures, blending until the dry ingredients are
   just moistened.
3. Spoon the batter into the prepared muffin cups, filling each about
   ¾ full. Bake for 15 to 20 minutes, or until the tops are golden and a
   cake tester or wooden toothpick inserted into the center of a muffin
   comes out clean. Cool in the pan on a wire rack for 5 to 7 minutes.
   Serve warm, or invert onto the rack
   to cool completely.

BUTTERNUT SQUASH
MUFFINS

makes 15 to 16 muffins

2 cups all-purpose flour
2 tbsp. granulated sugar
1 tbsp. baking powder
1 tsp. salt
1 large egg

1 cup milk
¼ cup butter or margarine,
  melted
⅔ cup cooked butternut
  squash, mashed

1. Position the rack in the center of the oven and preheat to 400 degrees.
   Lightly grease or line with paper baking cups sixteen 2¾-inch
   muffin cups.
2. In a large bowl, blend together the flour, sugar, baking powder,
   and salt. In a medium bowl, beat the egg, milk, butter, and mashed
   squash until smooth. Combine the two mixtures, blending until the
   dry ingredients are just moistened.
3. Spoon the batter into the prepared muffin cups, filling each about
   ¾ full. Bake for 15 to 20 minutes, or until a cake tester or wooden
   toothpick inserted into the center of a muffin comes out clean.
   Cool in the pan on a wire rack for 5 to 7 minutes. Serve warm,
   or invert onto the rack to cool completely.

CAJUN CORN MUFFINS

makes 11 to 12 muffins

1½ cups cornmeal
1½ cups all-purpose flour
3 tbsp. granulated sugar
1 tbsp. plus 1½ tsp. baking powder
1 tsp. cayenne pepper
1½ tsp. ground black pepper
½ cup seeded and diced red bell pepper

¼ cup seeded and diced green bell pepper
¼ cup finely minced yellow onion
1½ tsp. salt
2 large eggs
¼ cup canola oil
1 tbsp. butter or margarine, melted

1. Position the rack in the center of the oven and preheat to 400 degrees. Lightly grease or line with paper baking cups twelve 2¾-inch muffin cups.
2. In a large bowl, blend together the cornmeal, flour, sugar, baking powder, cayenne pepper, black pepper, bell peppers, onions, and salt. In a medium bowl, beat together the eggs, oil, and butter until smooth. Combine the two mixtures, blending until the dry ingredients are just moistened.
3. Spoon the batter into the prepared muffin cups, filling each about ¾ full. Bake for 15 to 20 minutes, or until a cake tester or wooden toothpick inserted into the center of a muffin comes out clean. Cool in the pan on a wire rack for 5 to 7 minutes. Serve warm, or invert onto the rack to cool completely.

CHEDDAR CHEESE-AND-PEPPER MUFFINS
makes 11 to 12 muffins

2 cups all-purpose flour
1 cup (4 oz.) shredded sharp
  Cheddar cheese
1 tbsp. granulated sugar
1 tbsp. baking powder

1½ tsp. ground white pepper
½ tsp. salt
1 large egg
¼ cup canola oil
1¼ cups milk

1. Position the rack in the center of the oven and preheat to 400 degrees. Lightly grease or line with paper baking cups twelve 2¾-inch muffin cups.
2. In a large bowl, blend together the flour, ¾ cup of the cheese, sugar, baking powder, pepper, and salt. In a medium bowl, beat the egg, oil, and milk until smooth. Combine the two mixtures, blending until the dry ingredients are just moistened.
3. Spoon the batter into the prepared muffin cups, filling each about ¾ full. Bake for 10 minutes. Sprinkle the remaining ¼ cup of cheese over the tops of the muffins and continue to bake for 5 to 10 minutes more, or until a cake tester or wooden toothpick inserted into the center of a muffin comes out clean. Cool in the pan on a wire rack for 5 to 7 minutes. Serve warm, or invert onto the rack to cool completely.

CHERRY
MUFFINS

makes 5 to 6 muffins

2 cups all-purpose flour
1 tbsp. baking powder
1 cup (16 oz.) pitted
  sweet black cherry halves
¼ tsp. salt
2 large eggs

⅔ cup granulated sugar
6 tbsp. butter or margarine,
  melted
½ cup milk
1 tsp. vanilla extract

1. Position the rack in the center of the oven and preheat to 400 degrees.
   Lightly grease or line with paper baking cups six 2¾-inch muffin cups.
2. In a large bowl, blend together the flour, baking powder, cherries,
   and salt. In a medium bowl, beat the eggs, butter, sugar, milk,
   and vanilla extract until smooth. Combine the two mixtures, blending
   until the dry ingredients are just moistened.
3. Spoon the batter into the prepared muffin cups, filling each about
   ¾ full. Bake for 15 to 20 minutes, or until a cake tester or wooden
   toothpick inserted into the center of a muffin comes out clean.
   Cool in the pan on a wire rack for 5 to 7 minutes. Serve warm,
   or invert onto the rack to cool completely.

COFFEE-GINGER MUFFINS

makes 23 to 24 muffins

1¾ cups all-purpose flour
½ cup granulated sugar
1 tsp. baking soda
¼ tsp. ground ginger
½ tsp. ground cardamom
¼ tsp. salt

1 large egg
½ cup molasses
½ cup strong brewed coffee
¼ cup butter or margarine,
    melted

1. Position the rack in the center of the oven and preheat to 375 degrees.
   Lightly grease or line with paper baking cups twenty-four 2¾-inch
   muffin cups.
2. In a large bowl, blend together the flour, sugar, baking soda, ginger,
   cardamom, and salt. In a medium bowl, beat the egg, molasses,
   coffee, and butter until smooth. Combine the two mixtures, blending
   until the dry ingredients are just moistened.
3. Spoon the batter into the prepared muffin cups, filling each about
   ¾ full. Bake for 15 to 20 minutes, or until a cake tester or wooden
   toothpick inserted into the center of a muffin comes out clean.
   Cool in the pan on a wire rack for 5 to 7 minutes. Serve warm,
   or invert onto the rack to cool completely.

CRANBERRY MUFFINS

makes 14 to 16 muffins

2 cups all-purpose flour
¾ cup granulated sugar
1 tbsp. baking powder
½ tsp. salt
1 large egg

1 cup milk
¼ cup butter or margarine, melted
1 cup chopped dried cranberries

1. Position the rack in the center of the oven and preheat to 400 degrees. Lightly grease or line with paper baking cups sixteen 2¾-inch muffin cups.
2. In a large bowl, blend together the flour, sugar, baking powder, and salt. In a medium bowl, beat the egg, milk, and butter until smooth. Fold in the cranberries. Combine the two mixtures, blending until the dry ingredients are just moistened.
3. Spoon the batter into the prepared muffin cups, filling each about ¾ full. Bake for 15 to 20 minutes, or until a cake tester or wooden toothpick inserted into the center of a muffin comes out clean. Cool in the pan on a wire rack for 5 to 7 minutes. Serve warm, or invert onto the rack to cool completely.

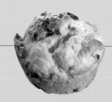

CREAM CHEESE-FILLED MUFFINS WITH RASPBERRIES

makes 12 muffins

2 cups all-purpose flour
1 tbsp. baking powder
2 tbsp. granulated sugar
½ tsp. salt
1 large egg

1 cup milk
¼ cup canola oil
1 package (8 oz.) cream
    cheese, cut into 12 chunks
28 to 32 raspberries

1. Position the rack in the center of the oven and preheat to 425 degrees. Lightly grease or line with paper baking cups twelve 2¾-inch muffin cups.

2. In a large bowl, blend together the flour, baking powder, sugar, and salt. In a small bowl, beat the egg until foamy. Beat in the milk and oil. Combine the two mixtures, blending until the dry ingredients are just moistened.

3. Spoon 1 heaping tablespoon of the batter into the prepared muffin cups. Press a cube of cream cheese into the center of each and top with two raspberries. Spoon a second tablespoon of the remaining batter on top of the raspberries. Bake for 15 to 20 minutes, or until a cake tester or wooden toothpick inserted near the edge of a muffin (not into the cream cheese) comes out clean. Cool in the pan on a wire rack for 5 to 7 minutes. Serve warm, or invert onto the rack to cool completely.

FRESH PEACH
MUFFINS

makes 11 to 12 muffins

1 cup chopped fresh peaches
  or fresh apricots
1 tsp. lemon juice
⅔ cup granulated sugar
2 cups all-purpose flour
1 tbsp. baking powder

½ tsp. ground cinnamon
1 large egg
1 cup milk
¼ cup butter or margarine,
  melted

1. Position the rack in the center of the oven and preheat to 450 degrees.
   Lightly grease or line with paper baking cups twelve 2¾-inch muffin cups.
2. Place the peaches in a small bowl and sprinkle them with lemon juice
   and 1 tablespoon of the sugar. Set aside. In a large bowl, blend
   together the flour, remaining sugar, baking powder, and cinnamon.
   In a medium bowl, beat the egg until thick and light-colored.
   Beat in the milk and margarine. Stir in the peaches. Combine the
   two mixtures, blending until the dry ingredients are just moistened.
3. Spoon the batter into the prepared muffin cups, filling each about
   ¾ full. Bake for 15 to 20 minutes, or until a cake tester or wooden
   toothpick inserted into the center of a muffin comes out clean.
   Cool in the pan on a wire rack for 5 to 7 minutes. Serve warm,
   or invert onto the rack to cool completely.

FRUIT-FILLED MUFFINS

makes 6 to 8 muffins

2 cups biscuit baking mix
2 tbsp. granulated sugar
⅔ cup skim milk
1 tbsp. canola oil

¼ cup cholesterol-free egg
  product
1 tbsp. Amaretto liqueur
¼ cup fruit preserves

1. Position the rack in the center of the oven and preheat to 400 degrees. Lightly grease or line with paper baking cups eight 2¾-inch muffin cups.
2. In a large bowl, blend together the baking mix and sugar. In a medium bowl, beat the milk, oil, Amaretto, and egg product until smooth. Combine the two mixtures, blending until the dry ingredients are just moistened.
3. Spoon the batter into the prepared muffin cups, filling each about ¾ full. Using a small spoon, divide the fruit preserves evenly between the cups into the center of each muffin. Bake for 15 to 20 minutes, or until a cake tester or wooden toothpick inserted at the edge of a muffin (not into the preserves) comes out clean. Cool in the pan on a wire rack for 5 to 7 minutes. Serve warm, or invert onto the rack to cool completely.

GINGER-AND-MOLASSES MUFFINS

makes 29 to 30 muffins

3 cups all-purpose flour
½ cup graham flour
1½ tsp. baking powder
1 tsp. baking soda
2 tsp. ground allspice
¼ cup finely chopped fresh,
  peeled ginger root
¼ tsp. salt

¼ cup finely chopped pecans
1 cup golden raisins (optional)
4 large eggs, separated
1 cup granulated sugar
½ cup butter or margarine,
  melted
1 cup molasses
1 cup sour milk or buttermilk

1. Position the rack in the center of the oven and preheat to 375 degrees.
   Lightly grease or line with paper baking cups thirty 2¾-inch muffin cups.

2. In a large bowl, blend together the two flours, baking powder,
   baking soda, allspice, ginger, salt, pecans, and raisins. In a medium
   bowl, beat the egg whites until stiff but not dry. Beat in the sugar,
   butter, molasses, and buttermilk. Combine the two mixtures, blending
   until the dry ingredients are just moistened.

3. Spoon the batter into the prepared muffin cups, filling each about
   ¾ full. Bake for 15 to 20 minutes, or until a cake tester or wooden
   toothpick inserted into the center of a muffin comes out clean.
   Cool in the pan on a wire rack for 5 to 7 minutes. Serve warm,
   or invert onto the rack to cool completely.

HONEY-CURRANT MUFFINS

makes 11 to 12 muffins

1¾ cups all-purpose flour
¼ cup graham flour
1 tbsp. baking powder
½ cup currants
1 tsp. salt
1 large egg

1 cup milk
¼ cup honey
2 tbsp. Amaretto liqueur
¼ cup butter or margarine,
  melted

1. Position the rack in the center of the oven and preheat to 400 degrees. Lightly grease or line with paper baking cups twelve 2¾-inch muffin cups.
2. In a large bowl, blend together the two flours, baking powder, currants, and salt. In a medium bowl, beat the egg, milk, honey, Amaretto, and butter until smooth. Combine the two mixtures, blending until the dry ingredients are just moistened.
3. Spoon the batter into the prepared muffin cups, filling each about ¾ full. Bake for 15 to 20 minutes, or until a cake tester or wooden toothpick inserted into the center of a muffin comes out clean. Cool in the pan on a wire rack for 5 to 7 minutes. Serve warm, or invert onto the rack to cool completely.

LEMON-AND-POPPY SEED MUFFINS

makes 11 to 12 muffins

1¾ cups all-purpose flour
⅓ cup plus 2 tbsp.
  granulated sugar
2 tsp. baking powder
2 tbsp. grated
  lemon zest

¼ tsp. salt
1 large egg
3 tbsp. canola oil
1 tbsp. plus 2 tsp. poppy seeds
1 cup milk
1 tbsp. lemon juice

1. Position the rack in the center of the oven and preheat to 400 degrees.
   Lightly grease or line with paper baking cups twelve 2¾-inch muffin cups.
2. In a large bowl, blend together the flour, ⅓ cup of the sugar,
   the baking powder, lemon zest, and salt. In a medium bowl,
   beat together the remaining 2 tablespoons of sugar, the egg, oil,
   1 tablespoon of the poppy seeds, the milk, and lemon juice.
   Combine the two mixtures, blending until the dry ingredients are just
   moistened.
3. Spoon the batter into the prepared muffin cups, filling each about
   ¾ full. Sprinkle the remaining 2 teaspoons of poppy seeds over the
   tops of the muffins. Bake for 15 to 20 minutes, or until a cake tester
   or wooden toothpick inserted into the center of a muffin comes out
   clean. Cool in the pan on a wire rack for 5 to 7 minutes. Serve warm,
   or invert onto the rack to cool completely.

MAPLE-BRAN
MUFFINS

makes 5 to 6 muffins

1½ cups whole-wheat flour
¾ cup wheat bran
1 tbsp. baking powder
⅓ cup chopped walnuts
½ tsp. salt

1 large egg
½ cup milk
¼ cup canola oil
½ cup maple syrup

1. Position the rack in the center of the oven and preheat to 400 degrees. Lightly grease or line with paper baking cups six 2¾-inch muffin cups.
2. In a large bowl, blend together the flour, bran, baking powder, walnuts, and salt. In a medium bowl, beat the egg, milk, oil, and maple syrup until smooth. Combine the two mixtures, blending until the dry ingredients are just moistened.
3. Spoon the batter into the prepared muffin cups, filling each about ¾ full. Bake for 15 to 20 minutes, or until a cake tester or wooden toothpick inserted into the center of a muffin comes out clean. Cool in the pan on a wire rack for 5 to 7 minutes. Serve warm, or transfer to the rack to cool completely.

MARMALADE-ALMOND MUFFINS

makes 11 to 12 muffins

2 cups all-purpose flour
3 tbsp. baking powder
⅔ cup granulated sugar
2 tbsp. grated
  orange zest
1 cup ground almonds

2 large eggs
¼ cup butter or margarine,
  melted
½ cup milk
⅔ cup orange marmalade
¼ cup slivered almonds

1. Position the rack in the center of the oven and preheat to 375 degrees.
   Lightly grease or line with paper baking cups twelve 2¾-inch muffin cups.
2. In a large bowl, blend together the flour, baking powder, sugar,
   orange zest, and ground almonds. In a medium bowl, beat the
   eggs until foamy. Beat in the butter and milk. Stir in the marmalade.
   Combine the two mixtures, blending until the dry ingredients are
   just moistened.
3. Spoon the batter into the prepared muffin cups, filling each about
   ¾ full. Sprinkle the slivered almonds over the tops of the muffins.
   Bake for 15 to 20 minutes, or until a cake tester or wooden toothpick
   inserted into the center of a muffin comes out clean. Cool in the pan
   on a wire rack for 5 to 7 minutes. Serve warm, or invert onto the rack
   to cool completely.

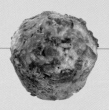

PARMESAN MUFFINS

makes 11 to 12 muffins

2 cups all-purpose flour
1½ tsp. baking powder
½ tsp. baking soda
½ cup grated Parmesan cheese
½ cup chopped fresh parsley
½ tsp. dried crushed marjoram

¼ cup butter or margarine,
  melted
1 tbsp. granulated sugar
1¼ cups buttermilk
  or sour milk
1 large egg

1. Position the rack in the center of the oven and preheat to 400 degrees.
   Lightly grease or line with paper baking cups twelve 2¾-inch muffin cups.
2. In large bowl, blend together the flour, baking powder, baking soda,
   parsley, cheese, and marjoram. In a medium bowl, beat the butter,
   sugar, buttermilk, and egg until smooth. Combine the two mixtures,
   blending until the dry ingredients are just moistened.
3. Spoon the batter into the prepared muffin cups, filling each about
   ¾ full. Bake for 15 to 20 minutes, or until a cake tester or wooden
   toothpick inserted into the center of a muffin comes out clean.
   Cool in the pan on a wire rack for 5 to 7 minutes. Serve warm,
   or invert onto the rack to cool completely.

SPICED SWEET POTATO MUFFINS

makes 11 to 12 muffins

¾ cup white corn flour
⅔ cup all-purpose flour
½ cup granulated sugar
2 tbsp. baking powder
1 tsp. baking soda
1½ tsp. pumpkin-pie spice
½ cup seedless raisins
½ cup chopped pecans
½ tsp. salt

2 large eggs
2 tbsp. butter or margarine,
   at room temperature
⅔ cup sour milk or buttermilk
1 tbsp. coffee-flavored liqueur
   or strong brewed coffee
1 tsp. almond extract
2 cups peeled cooked sweet
   potatoes, mashed

1. Position the rack in the center of the oven and preheat to 400 degrees.
   Lightly grease or line with paper baking cups twelve 2¾-inch muffin cups.
2. In a large bowl, blend together the two flours, sugar, baking powder,
   baking soda, pumpkin-pie spice, raisins, pecans, and salt. In a
   medium bowl, beat the eggs until thick and light-colored. Beat in the
   butter, milk, liqueur, almond extract, and potatoes. Combine the two
   mixtures, blending until the dry ingredients are just moistened.
3. Spoon the batter into the prepared muffin cups, filling each about
   ¾ full. Bake for 15 to 20 minutes, or until a cake tester or wooden
   toothpick inserted into the center of a muffin comes out clean.
   Cool in the pan on a wire rack for 5 to 7 minutes. Serve warm,
   or invert onto the rack to cool completely.

STRAWBERRY MUFFINS

makes 12 to 14 muffins

2¼ cups all-purpose flour
⅓ cup granulated sugar
1 tbsp. baking powder
½ tsp. salt

2 large eggs
½ cup milk
1 tsp. vanilla extract
1 cup sliced strawberries

1. Position the rack in the center of the oven and preheat to 400 degrees. Lightly grease or line with paper baking cups fourteen 2¾-inch muffin cups.
2. In a large bowl, blend together the flour, sugar, baking powder, and salt. In a medium bowl, beat the eggs until thick and light-colored. Beat in the milk and vanilla extract. Stir in the strawberries. Combine the two mixtures, blending until the dry ingredients are just moistened.
3. Spoon the batter into the prepared muffin cups, filling each about ¾ full. Bake for about 15 to 20 minutes, or until a cake tester or wooden toothpick inserted into the center of a muffin comes out clean. Cool in the pan on a wire rack for 5 to 7 minutes. Serve warm, or invert onto the rack to cool completely.

SWEET POTATO-AND-
MARSHMALLOW SURPRISE MUFFINS

makes 24 to 26 muffins

3 cups all-purpose flour
2 tsp. baking powder
1½ tsp. baking soda
1 cup granulated sugar
2 tsp. ground black pepper
½ tsp. salt

3 large eggs
½ cup milk
1 cup plus 2 tbsp. canola oil
2 cups (about 2) mashed
   cooked sweet potatoes
80 miniature marshmallows

1. Position the rack in the center of the oven and preheat to 375 degrees.
   Lightly grease or line with paper baking cups twenty-six 2¾-inch
   muffin cups.
2. In a large bowl, blend together the flour, baking powder, baking
   soda, sugar, pepper, and salt. In a medium bowl, beat the eggs until
   foamy. Beat in the milk, oil, and sweet potatoes. Combine the two
   mixtures, blending until the dry ingredients are just moistened.
3. Drop 1 heaping tablespoon of the batter into each of the prepared
   muffin cups. Press two miniature marshmallows into the batter in
   each cup and top each with 1 heaping tablespoon of the remaining
   batter. (The muffin cups should be about ⅔ full). Press one or more
   miniature marshmallows onto the top of each muffin.
4. Bake for 15 to 20 minutes, or until a cake tester or wooden toothpick
   inserted into the edge of a muffin (not into the marshmallows)
   comes out clean. Cool in the pan on a wire rack for 5 to 7 minutes.
   Serve warm, or invert onto the rack to cool completely.

YANKEE MAPLE
MUFFINS

makes 12 to 14 muffins

2 cups all-purpose flour
1 cup yellow cornmeal
1 tbsp. baking powder
2 large eggs
¼ cup packed light-brown
  sugar

1 cup milk
⅓ cup maple syrup
¼ cup butter or margarine,
  melted
½ cup crushed, canned
  pineapple, drained

1. Position the rack in the center of the oven and preheat to 375 degrees.
   Lightly grease or line with paper baking cups fourteen 2¾-inch
   muffin cups.
2. In a large bowl, blend together the flour, cornmeal, and baking
   powder. In a medium bowl, beat the eggs until foamy. Beat in the
   sugar. Beat in the milk, syrup, butter, and pineapple. Combine the
   two mixtures, blending until the dry ingredients are just moistened.
3. Spoon the batter into the prepared muffin cups, filling each about
   ¾ full. Bake for 25 to 30 minutes, or until a cake tester or wooden
   toothpick inserted into the center of a muffin comes out clean.
   Remove from the oven and brush the top of each muffin with the
   melted butter. Cool in the pan on a wire rack for 5 to 7 minutes.
   Serve warm, or invert onto the rack to cool completely.

ZUCCHINI MUFFINS

makes 23 to 24 muffins

2 cups all-purpose flour
1 cup granulated sugar
1 tsp. baking soda
¼ tsp. baking powder
1½ tsp. ground cinnamon
1 cup golden raisins

½ cup chopped walnuts
½ tsp. salt
2 large eggs
½ cup canola oil
1 tbsp. vanilla extract
2 cups shredded zucchini

1. Position the rack in the center of the oven and preheat to 375 degrees. Lightly grease or line with paper baking cups twenty-four 2¾-inch muffin cups.

2. In a large bowl, blend together the flour, sugar, baking soda, baking powder, cinnamon, raisins, walnuts, and salt. In a medium bowl, beat the eggs until foamy. Beat in the oil and vanilla extract. Stir in zucchini. Combine the two mixtures, blending until the dry ingredients are just moistened.

3. Spoon the batter into the prepared muffin cups, filling each about ¾ full. Bake for 15 to 20 minutes, or until a cake tester or wooden toothpick inserted into the center of a muffin comes out clean. Cool in the pan on a wire rack for 5 to 7 minutes. Serve warm, or invert onto the rack to cool completely.

APPLESAUCE
BISCUITS

makes 6 to 8 biscuits

2 cups all-purpose flour
1 tbsp. baking powder
¼ tsp. baking soda
1 tsp. salt
3 tbsp. vegetable shortening,
  chilled

1 large egg
¼ cup sour cream
½ cup applesauce
½ cup grated cheese

1. Position the rack in the center of the oven and preheat to 425 degrees.
2. In a large bowl, blend together the flour, baking powder, baking
   soda, and salt. Using a pastry blender or two knives scissor-fashion,
   cut in the shortening until the mixture resembles fine meal. In a small
   bowl, combine the egg, sour cream, and applesauce. (Do not beat.)
   Pour into the dry mixture all at one time and stir briefly until the
   dough holds together.
3. Turn the dough out onto a lightly floured surface and knead 7 to 8
   times. Using a rolling pin, roll the dough out to a thickness of ½ inch.
   Using a 2-inch round cutter, cut out as many biscuits as possible.
   Place the biscuits 1 inch apart on an ungreased baking sheet.
   Rework the scraps until all the biscuits are cut.
4. Sprinkle the cheese over the top of the biscuits and bake for 10 to 12
   minutes, or until the tops are golden brown. Serve warm.

QUICK CHEESE BISCUITS

makes 4 to 6 biscuits

2¼ cups biscuit baking mix
⅔ cup white port wine

1½ cups shredded sharp
Cheddar cheese

1. Position the rack in the center of the oven and preheat to 425 degrees.
2. In a large bowl, combine the baking mix and wine and stir just until the dough holds together. (Do not overmix.) Stir in the cheese.
3. Turn the dough out onto a lightly floured surface and knead 7 to 8 times. Using a rolling pin, roll the dough out to a thickness of ½ inch. Using a 2-inch round cutter, cut out as many biscuits as possible. Place the biscuits 1 inch apart on an ungreased baking sheet. Rework the scraps until all the dough is used and brush with the remaining butter. Bake for 10 to 12 minutes, or until the tops of the biscuits are golden brown. Serve warm.

BLACKBERRY
BISCUITS

makes 6 to 8 biscuits

1 cup all-purpose flour
¼ cup graham flour
1½ tsp. baking powder
¼ cup granulated sugar
½ tsp. salt

¼ cup heavy cream
½ cup berry-flavored yogurt
½ cup blackberries
   washed and dried

1. Position the rack in the center of the oven and preheat to 425 degrees.
2. In a large bowl, blend together the two flours, baking powder, sugar,
   salt, cream, and yogurt, stirring just until the dough holds together.
   (Do not overmix.) Stir in the blackberries.
3. Turn the dough out onto a lightly floured surface and knead 7 to
   8 times. Using a rolling pin, roll the dough out to a thickness of
   ½ inch. Using a 2-inch round cutter, cut out as many biscuits as
   possible. Place the biscuits 1 inch apart on an ungreased baking
   sheet. Rework the scraps until all the dough is used. Bake for 10 to
   12 minutes, or until the tops of the biscuits are golden brown.
   Serve warm.

BUTTERMILK BISCUITS

makes 10 to 12 biscuits

2 cups all-purpose flour
2½ tsp. baking powder
¼ tsp. baking soda
1 tbsp. granulated sugar
¼ tsp. salt

6 tbsp. butter or margarine, chilled
¼ cup melted butter or margarine, melted (for brushing)
¾ cup buttermilk or sour milk

1. Position the rack in the center of the oven and preheat to 425 degrees.
2. In a large bowl, blend together the flour, baking powder, baking soda, sugar, and salt. Using a pastry blender or two knives scissor-fashion, cut in the butter until the mixture resembles fine meal. Add the buttermilk all at one time and stir just until the dough holds together. (Do not overmix.)
3. Turn the dough out onto a lightly floured surface and knead 7 to 8 times. Using a rolling pin, roll the dough out to a thickness of ½ inch. Using a 2-inch round cutter, cut out as many biscuits as possible. Place the biscuits 1 inch apart on an ungreased baking sheet. Rework the scraps until all the dough is used. Brush with the melted butter. Bake for 10 to 12 minutes, or until the tops of the biscuits are golden brown. Serve warm.

CAMP
BISCUITS
makes 16 to 18 biscuits

2 cups all-purpose flour
3¾ tsp. baking powder
1 tsp. salt

6 tbsp. butter or margarine,
   at room temperature
¾ cup milk

1. Lightly grease a skillet and preheat it over a low flame.
2. In a large bowl, blend together the flour, baking powder, and salt.
   Using a pastry blender or two knives scissor-fashion, cut in the butter
   until the mixture resembles fine meal. Add the milk all at one time
   and stir just until the dough holds together. (Do not overmix.)
3. Turn the dough out onto a lightly floured surface and knead 7 to 8
   times. Using a rolling pin, roll the dough out to a thickness of ½ inch.
   Using a 2-inch round cutter or the top of a cup or glass, cut out as
   many biscuits as possible. Place the biscuits 1 inch apart on the
   prepared skillet (you may have to work in batches). Cook until the
   biscuits are light brown on the underside. Turn and brown on the
   other side. Serve at once.

CHEDDAR CHEESE BISCUITS

makes 6 to 8 biscuits

2 cups all-purpose flour
4 tsp. baking powder
2 tsp. granulated sugar
½ tsp. salt
2 tbsp. butter or margarine,
  at room temperature

1 large egg
¾ cup milk
½ cup grated Cheddar cheese

1. Position the rack in the center of the oven and preheat to 425 degrees.
2. In a large bowl, blend together the flour, baking powder, sugar,
   and salt. In a medium bowl, beat the egg, butter, and milk together
   before stirring in the Cheddar cheese. Then combine the two mixes,
   blending just until the dough holds together. (Do not overmix.)
3. Turn the dough out onto a lightly floured surface and knead 7 to 8
   times. Using a rolling pin, roll the dough out to a thickness of ½ inch.
   Cut with a 1-inch round cutter. Place the biscuits 1 inch apart on
   an ungreased baking sheet. Rework the scraps until all the dough is
   used. Bake for 10 to 12 minutes, or until the tops of the biscuits are
   golden brown. Serve warm.

CHOPPED CHERRY
BISCUITS

makes 8 to 10 biscuits

1½ cups all-purpose flour
1 tbsp. baking powder
1½ tsp. granulated sugar
½ tsp. cream of tartar
¼ cup finely chopped
  dried cherries

½ tsp. salt
¼ cup vegetable shortening,
  chilled
½ cup milk
¾ cup butter or margarine,
  melted

1. Position the rack in the center of the oven and preheat to 425 degrees.
2. In a large bowl, blend together the flour, baking powder, chopped dried cherries, sugar, salt, and cream of tartar. Using a pastry blender or two knives scissor-fashion, cut in the shortening until the mixture resembles fine meal. Pour the milk and ½ cup of the butter in all at one time and stir just until the dough holds together. (Do not overmix.)
3. Turn the dough out onto a lightly floured surface and knead 7 to 8 times. Using a rolling pin, roll the dough out to a thickness of ½ inch. Using a 2-inch round cutter, cut out as many biscuits as possible. Place the biscuits 1 inch apart on an ungreased baking sheet. Rework the scraps until all the dough is used and brush with the remaining butter. Bake for 12 to 15 minutes, or until the tops of the biscuits are golden brown. Serve warm.

GREEN TOMATO
BISCUITS

makes 14 to 16 biscuits

1 cup all-purpose flour	½ cup chopped green
1 cup whole-wheat flour	tomatoes
1 tbsp. baking powder	1 tsp. wine vinegar
¼ cup grated Romano cheese	6 tbsp. butter or margarine,
¾ tsp. salt	melted
2 large eggs	

1. Position the rack in the center of the oven and preheat to 425 degrees.
2. In a large bowl, blend together the two flours, baking powder, cheese, and salt. In a medium bowl, blend together the egg, green tomatoes, vinegar, and butter. Then combine the two mixtures, blending until the dry ingredients are just moistened. (Do not overmix.)
3. Turn the dough out onto a lightly floured surface and knead 7 to 8 times. Using a rolling pin, roll the dough out to a thickness of ½ inch. Using a 2-inch round cutter, cut out as many biscuits as possible. Place the biscuits 1 inch apart on an ungreased baking sheet. Rework the scraps until all the dough is used. Bake for 10 to 12 minutes, or until the tops of the biscuits are golden brown. Serve warm.

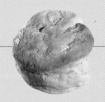

HEAVY CREAM
BISCUITS
makes 4 to 6 biscuits

1¾ cups all-purpose flour   1 cup heavy cream
2½ tsp. baking powder   ½ tsp. salt

1. Position the rack in the center of the oven and preheat to 450 degrees.
2. In a large bowl, combine the flour, baking powder, cream, and salt
   and stir just until the dough holds together. (Do not overmix.)
3. Turn the dough out onto a lightly floured surface and knead 7 or 8
   times. Using a rolling pin, roll the dough out to a thickness of ½ inch.
   Using a 2-inch round cutter, cut out as many biscuits as possible.
   Place the biscuits 1 inch apart on an ungreased baking sheet.
   Rework the scraps until all the dough is used. Bake for 10 to 12
   minutes, or until the top of the biscuits are golden brown. Serve warm.

HONEY
BISCUITS

makes 10 to 12 biscuits

⅓ cup butter or margarine, at room temperature
¼ cup honey
2 cups all-purpose flour
4 tsp. baking powder

½ tbsp. salt
¼ cup butter, or margarine at room temperature
⅔ cup milk
¼ cup sesame seeds

1. Position the rack in the center of the oven and preheat to 325 degrees.
2. To make the filling, in a small bowl, beat together the butter and honey until smooth. Set aside.
3. To make the dough, in a large bowl, blend together the flour, baking powder, and salt. Work in the butter until the mixture resembles fine meal. Add the milk all at one time and stir just until the dough holds together. (Do not overmix.)
4. Turn the dough out onto a lightly floured surface and knead 7 to 8 times. Roll out to a rectangle ½ inch thick. Brush the rectangle with the honey butter. Roll the rectangle up jelly-roll fashion and cut into 1-inch slices. Place the slices on an ungreased baking sheet, and brush with any remaining honey butter. Sprinkle the tops of the biscuits with sesame seeds. Bake for 10 to 12 minutes, or until the tops of the biscuits are golden brown. Serve warm.

JALAPEÑO PEPPER-CHEESE BISCUITS

makes 6 biscuits

1 cup all-purpose flour
2 tbsp. cornmeal
1½ tsp. baking powder
½ cup finely grated sharp
Cheddar cheese
2 tbsp. peeled and
chopped tomato

1 tsp. seeded, minced
jalapeño pepper
½ tsp. salt
½ cup milk

1. Position the rack in the center of the oven and preheat to 425 degrees.
2. In a large bowl, blend together the flour, cornmeal, baking powder, cheese, tomatoes, peppers, and salt. Add the milk all at one time and stir just until the dough holds together. (Do not overmix.)
3. Turn the dough out onto a lightly floured surface and knead 7 to 8 times. Divide the dough into 6 equal balls and place the balls on an ungreased baking sheet. Pat the balls into 3-inch rounds. Bake for 10 to 12 minutes, or until the tops of the biscuits are golden brown. Serve warm.

MASHED POTATO BISCUITS

makes 10 to 12 biscuits

1¾ cups all-purpose flour	4 large egg yolks
1 tsp. salt	2 tbsp. sour cream
½ cup chilled butter	1 cup cold mashed potatoes

1 Position the rack in the center of the oven and preheat to 425 degrees.
2 In a large bowl, blend together the flour and salt. Using a pastry
   blender or two knives scissor-fashion, cut in the butter until the
   mixture resembles fine meal. In a medium bowl, beat 3 of the egg
   yolks until foamy before beating in the sour cream and potatoes.
   Combine the two mixtures, blending until the dry ingredients are
   just moistened and the dough holds together. (Do not overmix.)
3 Turn the dough out onto a lightly floured surface and knead 7 to 8
   times. Using a rolling pin, roll the dough out to a thickness of ½ inch.
   Using a 2-inch round cutter, cut out as many biscuits as possible.
   Place the biscuits 1 inch apart on an ungreased baking sheet. Rework
   the scraps until all the dough is used. Brush the tops of the biscuits
   with the remaining egg yolk. Bake for 10 to 12 minutes, or until the
   tops of the biscuits are golden brown. Serve warm.

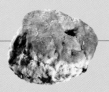

PATRIOTIC
BISCUITS

makes 10 to 12 biscuits

2 cups all-purpose flour
1 tbsp. baking powder
2 tbsp. granulated sugar
½ tsp. salt
½ cup butter or margarine,
  at room temperature

¼ cup finely chopped
  cranberries
¼ cup finely chopped
  blueberries
1 large egg, lightly beaten
½ cup milk

1. Position the rack in the center of the oven and preheat to 425 degrees.
2. In a large bowl, blend together the flour, baking powder, sugar, and salt. Work in the butter until the mixture resembles fine meal. Stir in the cranberries and blueberries. Add the egg and milk all at one time, and stir just until the dough holds together. (Do not overmix.)
3. Turn the dough out onto a lightly floured surface and knead 7 to 8 times. Using a rolling pin, roll the dough out to a thickness of ½ inch. Using a 2-inch round cutter, cut out as many biscuits as possible. Place the biscuits 1 inch apart on an ungreased baking sheet. Rework the scraps until all the dough is used. Bake for 10 to 12 minutes, or until the tops of the biscuits are golden brown. Serve warm.

PEPPER EGG
BISCUITS

makes 10 to 12 biscuits

3 cups all-purpose flour
4½ tsp. baking powder
1 tbsp. granulated sugar
¾ tsp. salt
½ cup chilled butter
   or margarine

1 large bell pepper, seeded
   and finely diced
1 large egg
¾ cup milk

1. Position the rack in the center of the oven and preheat to 425 degrees.
2. In a large bowl, blend together the flour, baking powder, sugar, and
   salt. Using a pastry blender or two knives scissor-fashion, cut in the
   butter until the mixture resembles fine meal. Stir in the pepper. In a
   small bowl, whisk together the egg and milk. Combine the two
   mixtures, blending just until the dough holds together. (Do not overmix.)
3. Turn the dough out onto a lightly floured surface and knead 7 to 8
   times. Using a rolling pin, roll the dough out to a thickness of ½ inch.
   Using a 2-inch round cutter, cut out as many biscuits as possible.
   Place the biscuits 1 inch apart on an ungreased baking sheet.
   Rework the scraps until all the dough is used. Bake for 10 to 12
   minutes, or until the tops of the biscuits are golden brown.
   Serve warm.

RUM
BISCUITS

makes 10 to 12 biscuits

2 cups all-purpose flour
2 tsp. baking powder
½ tsp. salt
3 tbsp. butter or
  margarine, chilled

¾ cup milk
12 sugar cubes
¼ cup rum

1. Position the rack in the center of the oven and preheat to 425 degrees.
2. In a large bowl, blend together the flour, baking powder, and salt.
   Using a pastry blender or two knives scissor-fashion, cut in the butter
   until the mixture resembles fine meal. Add the milk all at one time
   and stir just until the dough holds together. (Do not overmix.)
3. Turn the dough out onto a lightly floured surface and knead 7 to 8
   times. Using a rolling pin, roll the dough out to a thickness of ½ inch.
   Using a 2-inch round cutter, cut out as many biscuits as possible.
   Place the biscuits 1 inch apart on an ungreased baking sheet. Rework
   the scraps until all the dough is used. Push a sugar cube into the
   center of each biscuit. Spoon the rum evenly over the sugar cubes.
   Bake for 10 to 12 minutes, or until the tops of the biscuits are golden
   brown. Serve warm.

SUGARLESS WHOLE WHEAT BISCUITS

makes 8 to 10 biscuits

1½ cups all-purpose flour
½ cup whole-wheat flour
1 tbsp. baking powder
½ tsp. salt

⅓ cup vegetable shortening, chilled
¾ cup milk
Sesame seeds for sprinkling

1. Position the rack in the center of the oven and preheat to 425 degrees.
2. In a large bowl, blend together the two flours, baking powder, and salt. Using a pastry blender or two knives scissor-fashion, cut in the shortening until the mixture resembles fine meal. Add the milk all at one time and stir just until the dough holds together. (Do not overmix.)
3. Turn the dough out onto a lightly floured surface and knead 7 to 8 times. Using a rolling pin, roll the dough out to a thickness of ½ inch. Using a 2-inch round cutter, cut out as many biscuits as possible. Place the biscuits 1 inch apart on an ungreased baking sheet. Rework the scraps until all the dough is used. Sprinkle the tops of the biscuits with sesame seeds. Bake for 10 to 12 minutes, or until the tops of the biscuits are golden brown. Serve warm.

ALL-GRAIN
SCONES

makes 8 scones

½ cup buttermilk
1 large egg
1 tbsp. honey
1 tbsp. molasses
¼ cup unprocessed bran
½ cup all-purpose flour
½ cup whole-wheat flour
¼ cup rye flour

⅓ cup rolled oats
¼ cup cornmeal
2 tsp. baking powder
½ tsp. baking soda
½ tsp. salt
6 tbsp. chilled butter
   or margarine, diced

1. Position the rack in the center of the oven and preheat to 400 degrees.
   Lightly grease and flour a baking sheet.
2. In a medium bowl, beat the buttermilk, egg, honey, and molasses
   until smooth. Stir in the bran. In a large bowl, blend together the
   three flours, rolled oats, cornmeal, baking powder, baking soda,
   and salt. Using a pastry blender or two knives scissor-fashion,
   cut the butter into the mixture until it resembles coarse meal.
   Gently stir in the wet ingredients until the dough just holds together.
3. Transfer the dough to the prepared baking sheet and pat it into an
   8-inch circle. Using a serrated knife, score into 8 wedges (do not cut
   all the way through the dough). Bake for 18 to 20 minutes, or until
   the top is golden. Remove from the oven and serve hot.

APPLE-OATMEAL
SCONES

makes 8 scones

1½ cups all-purpose flour
1 cup rolled oats
2½ tsp. baking powder
⅓ cup packed brown sugar
½ tsp. salt
½ cup chilled butter or
  margarine, diced
¾ cup chopped apples,
  unpeeled and cored

⅔ cup chopped pitted dates
1 large egg, beaten
¼ cup milk, plus more
  for brushing the scones
2 tbsp. molasses
1 tsp. vanilla extract

1. Position the rack in the center of the oven and preheat to 400 degrees.
   Lightly grease and flour a baking sheet.
2. In a large bowl, blend together the oats, baking powder, brown
   sugar, and salt. Using a pastry blender or two knives scissor-fashion,
   cut the butter into the mixture until it resembles coarse meal. Stir in
   the apples and dates. Add the egg, milk, molasses, and vanilla
   extract, stirring gently until the dough just holds together.
3. Transfer the dough to the prepared baking sheet and pat it into an
   8-inch circle. Using a serrated knife, score the dough into 8 wedges
   (do not cut all the way through the dough). Brush the top of the
   scone with milk and bake for 18 to 20 minutes, or until the top is
   golden brown. Remove from the oven and serve hot.

AUNT ETHEL'S
ABERDEEN SCONES

makes 4 large scones

3 cups all-purpose flour
6 tsp. baking powder
6 tbsp. granulated sugar
1 tsp. salt

2 tbsp. chilled vegetable
  shortening
1 cup buttermilk
1 large egg, beaten

1. In a large bowl, blend together the flour, baking powder, sugar,
   and salt. Using a pastry blender or two knives scissor-fashion,
   cut in the shortening until the mixture forms fine crumbs. Add the
   buttermilk and egg, stirring gently until the dough holds together.
2. Turn the dough out onto a floured surface and pat it out to a
   thickness of ¾-inch. Cut the dough into four wedges.
3. Preheat a large skillet over medium heat. Place the pieces,
   one at a time, in the heated skillet and fry until browned on both
   sides. Remove from the pan and serve hot.

BLUE CHEESE-AND-GOLDEN RAISIN SCONES

makes 8 scones

1 cup all-purpose flour
2 tsp. baking powder
Dash of white pepper
¼ cup chilled butter or
  margarine

¼ cup crumbled blue cheese
¼ cup golden raisins
½ cup milk

1. Position the rack in the center of the oven and preheat to 425 degrees. Lightly grease and flour a baking sheet.
2. In a large bowl, blend together the flour, baking powder, and pepper. Using a pastry blender or two knives scissor-fashion, cut in the butter until the mixture resembles coarse meal. Stir in the cheese and raisins. Add the milk, stirring gently until the dough holds together.
3. Turn the dough out onto a lightly floured surface and knead a few times. Shape into a ball, place the ball on the prepared baking sheet, and pat into a ½-inch-thick circle. Using a serrated knife, score into 8 wedges (do not cut all the way through the dough). Bake for 10 to 15 minutes, or until golden brown. Remove from the oven and serve hot.

BUCKINGHAM PALACE
SCONES
makes 8 scones

3½ cups all-purpose flour
1 tbsp. baking powder
½ cup granulated sugar,
   plus more for sprinkling
   over the scones
Pinch salt

¾ cup chilled butter
   or margarine
½ cup raisins
1 large egg, beaten
½ cup milk
1 large egg white, beaten

1. Position the rack in the center of the oven and preheat to 350 degrees.
   Lightly grease and flour a baking sheet.
2. In a large bowl, blend together the flour, baking powder, ½ cup
   sugar, and salt. Using a pastry blender or two knives scissor-fashion,
   cut in the butter until the mixture resembles coarse meal. Stir in
   the raisins. Add the egg and milk, stirring gently until the dough
   holds together.
3. Turn the dough out onto the prepared baking sheet, and pat it into
   a ½-inch-thick circle. Using a serrated knife, score into 8 wedges
   (do not cut all the way through the dough). Brush with the beaten
   egg white and sprinkle with granulated sugar. Bake for 10 to 12
   minutes, or until the top is golden brown. Remove from the oven
   and serve hot.

CAPE BRETON
SCONES
makes 16 scones

2 cups all-purpose flour
1 tbsp. baking powder
¼ tsp. baking soda
2 tbsp. granulated sugar,
plus more for sprinkling
over the scones
1 tsp. salt

1 cup chopped raisins
or currants
½ cup sour cream or yogurt
¼ cup canola oil
1 large egg, beaten
3 tbsp. milk, plus more
for brushing the scones

1. Position the rack in the center of the oven and preheat to 425 degrees.
    Lightly grease and flour a baking sheet.
2. In a large bowl, blend together the flour, baking powder, baking soda,
    the 2 tablespoons of sugar, salt, raisins, sour cream, oil, egg, and the
    3 tablespoons of milk and stir gently until the dough holds together.
3. Turn the dough out onto a lightly floured surface and knead gently
    until no longer sticky. Divide into two equal parts and form each into
    a ball. Place the balls on the prepared baking sheet and pat them
    into 6-inch circles. Using a serrated knife, score each into 8 wedges
    (do not cut all the way through the dough). Brush the tops with milk
    and sprinkle with granulated sugar. Bake for 10 to 12 minutes, or
    until the tops are golden brown. Remove from the oven and serve hot.

CURRANT AND BRANDY
SCONES

makes 10 to 12 scones

1 cup dried currants	½ tsp. baking soda
3 tbsp. brandy	¼ cup granulated sugar
4 cups all-purpose flour	1 cup chilled butter
½ cup rice flour	or margarine, diced
2 tsp. baking powder	1 cup heavy cream

1. In a cup, combine the currants and brandy and set aside to soak.
   In a large bowl, blend together the two flours, baking powder,
   baking soda, and sugar. Using a pastry blender or two knives
   scissor-fashion, cut the butter into the dry ingredients until the
   mixture resembles coarse meal. Add the currants and cream,
   stirring gently until the dough holds together.
2. Gather the dough into a ball and wrap it in plastic wrap.
   Refrigerate until well chilled, about one hour.
3. When ready to bake, position the rack in the center of the oven
   and preheat to 400 degrees. Lightly grease and flour a baking sheet.
4. Unwrap the dough and turn it out onto a floured surface.
   Roll the dough out to a thickness of ½ inch. Using a biscuit cutter,
   cut into 2-inch circles, reworking the scraps as you go. Place the
   circles 1 inch apart on the prepared baking sheet. Bake for 13 to 15
   minutes, or until golden brown. Remove from the oven and serve hot.

ENGLISH CREAM
SCONES

makes 10 to 12 scones

2 cups all-purpose flour
1 tbsp. baking powder
4 tsp. granulated sugar,
   plus more for sprinkling
   over the scones
½ tsp. salt

¼ cup chilled butter
   or margarine, diced
2 large eggs, beaten
½ cup sweet cream
1 beaten egg white

1. Position the rack in the center of the oven and preheat to 375 degrees.
   Lightly grease and flour a baking sheet.
2. In a large bowl, blend together the flour, baking powder, the 4
   teaspoons of sugar, and the salt. Using a pastry blender or two
   knives scissor-fashion, cut in the butter until the mixture resembles
   coarse meal. Add the egg and cream, stirring gently until the dough
   holds together.
3. Turn the dough out onto a floured surface and knead several times
   before rolling out to a thickness of ½ inch. Using a biscuit cutter,
   cut the dough into 2-inch circles, reworking the scraps as you go.
   Place the circles 1 inch apart on the prepared baking sheet. Brush
   with the beaten egg white and sprinkle with sugar. Bake for 15 to 18
   minutes, or until golden brown. Remove from the oven and serve hot.

GINGER SCONES

makes 12 scones

2¾ cups all-purpose flour
3½ tsp. baking powder
½ cup granulated sugar
½ tsp. salt
6 tbsp. minced crystallized
  ginger

1⅔ cups heavy cream
¼ tsp. ground ginger
  for sprinkling
6 tbsp. granulated sugar
  for sprinkling

1. Position the rack in the center of the oven and preheat to 425 degrees.
   Lightly grease and flour a baking sheet.
2. To make the dough, in a large bowl, blend together the flour, baking
   powder, sugar, salt, crystallized ginger, and cream and stir gently until
   the dough holds together.
3. Turn the dough out onto a floured surface and knead several times
   before rolling out to a thickness of ½ inch. Using a biscuit cutter,
   cut the dough into 2-inch circles, reworking scraps as you go. Place
   the circles 1 inch apart on the prepared baking sheet.
4. To make the topping, in a cup, combine the ground ginger and
   sugar. Sprinkle over the tops of the scones and bake for 10 to 15
   minutes, or until golden brown. Remove from the oven and serve hot.

OLD-FASHIONED ORANGE SCONES

makes 8 scones

2 cups all-purpose flour
1 tbsp. baking powder
¼ cup powdered sugar
½ tsp. salt
¼ cup chilled butter
  or margarine

1 tsp. grated orange zest
¾ cup heavy cream
1 large egg, beaten
½ cup finely chopped
  golden raisins

1. Position the rack in the center of the oven and preheat to 350 degrees.
   Lightly grease and flour the bottom of a 6-inch round baking pan.
2. In a large bowl, blend together the flour, baking powder, sugar, and
   salt. Using a pastry blender or two knives scissor-fashion, cut in the
   butter until the mixture resembles coarse meal. Add the orange zest,
   cream, egg, and raisins and stir gently until the dough holds together.
3. Turn the dough out into the prepared baking pan and pat it down.
   Using a serrated knife, score the dough into 8 wedges (do not cut
   all the way through). Bake for 20 to 25 minutes, or until a golden
   brown. Remove from the oven and cool on a wire rack for about
   5 to 7 minutes before serving warm.

PARMESAN-AND-CHEDDAR CHEESE SCONES

makes 8 scones

2 cups all-purpose flour
2 tsp. baking powder
Dash of ground cayenne
 pepper
¼ tsp. salt
⅓ cup chilled butter
 or margarine, diced

3 tbsp. grated Parmesan cheese
1½ cups shredded
 Cheddar cheese
2 large eggs, beaten
⅓ cup milk

1. Position the rack in the center of the oven and preheat to 400 degrees. Lightly grease and flour a baking sheet.
2. In a large bowl, blend together the flour, baking powder, cayenne, and salt. Using a pastry blender or two knives scissor-fashion, cut in the butter until the mixture resembles coarse meal. Stir in the Parmesan and Cheddar cheese. Add the eggs and milk, stirring gently until the dough holds together.
3. Turn the dough out onto the prepared baking sheet and pat it into an 8-inch circle. Using a serrated knife, score the dough into 8 wedges (do not cut all the way through the dough). Bake for 15 to 18 minutes, or until a golden brown. Remove from the oven and cool on a wire rack for 5 to 7 minutes before serving warm.

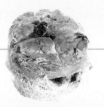

RAISIN
SCONES
makes 16 to 18 scones

3¼ cups all-purpose flour
1 tbsp. baking powder
5 tbsp. granulated sugar
1 tsp. salt

6 tbsp. chilled butter
  or margarine, diced
1 cup golden raisins
1 cup milk

1. Position the rack in the center of the oven and preheat to 425 degrees.
   Lightly grease and flour a baking sheet.
2. In a large bowl, blend together the flour, baking powder, sugar, and
   salt. Using a pastry blender or two knives scissor-fashion, cut in the
   butter until the mixture resembles coarse meal. Stir in the raisins.
   Add the milk and stir gently until the dough holds together.
3. Turn the dough out onto a floured surface and knead several times
   before rolling it out to a thickness of ½ inch. Using a biscuit cutter,
   cut the dough into 2-inch circles, placing the circles 1½ inches apart
   on the prepared baking sheet. Bake for 8 to 10 minutes or until
   golden brown. Remove from the oven and serve hot.

ROSEMARY SCONES

makes 8 scones

2¼ cups all-purpose flour
2 tsp. baking powder
¼ tsp. baking soda
1 tsp. salt
½ cup cold butter
  or margarine, diced

1 tsp. fresh minced rosemary
½ tsp. grated lemon zest
⅓ cup buttermilk
1 large egg

1. Position the rack in the center of the oven and preheat to 400 degrees. Lightly grease and flour a baking sheet.
2. In a large bowl, blend together the flour, baking powder, baking soda, and salt. Using a pastry blender or two knives scissor-fashion, cut in the butter until the mixture resembles coarse meal. Stir in the rosemary and lemon zest. In a small bowl, beat the buttermilk and egg until smooth. Combine the two mixtures, stirring gently until the dough holds together.
3. Gather the dough into a ball and place it on the prepared baking sheet. Pat the dough into an 8-inch circle. Using a serrated knife, cut the circle into 8 wedges, cutting all the way through the dough. Separate the wedges slightly and bake for 13 to 15 minutes, or until the tops are lightly browned. Remove from the oven and serve hot.

SCOTTISH OAT SCONES

makes 8 scones

1½ cups all-purpose flour
1¼ cups old-fashioned
  rolled oats
1 tbsp. baking powder
1 tsp. cream of tartar
¼ cup granulated sugar
½ tsp. ground nutmeg

½ tsp. salt
1 large egg, beaten
⅓ cup milk
⅔ cup melted butter
  or margarine
½ cup golden raisins

1. Position the rack in the center of the oven and preheat to 450 degrees. Lightly grease and flour a baking sheet.
2. In a large bowl, blend together the flour, oats, baking powder, cream of tartar, sugar, nutmeg, salt, egg, milk, butter, and raisins. Stir gently until the dough holds together.
3. Gather the dough into a ball and transfer it to the prepared baking sheet. Pat the dough out into a ¾-inch-thick circle. Using a serrated knife, score into 8 wedges (do not cut all the way through) and bake for 10 to 12 minutes, or until golden brown. Remove from the oven and cool on a wire rack for 5 to 7 minutes before serving warm.

WHOLE WHEAT SCONES

makes 4 scones

1 cup whole-wheat flour
⅓ cup all-purpose flour
½ tsp. baking powder
2 tbsp. wheat germ
2 tbsp. granulated sugar

¼ tsp. salt
¼ cup chilled butter
  or margarine, diced
½ cup milk

1. Position the rack in the center of the oven and preheat to 375 degrees.
   Lightly grease and flour a baking sheet.
2. In a large bowl, blend together the two flours, baking powder,
   wheat germ, sugar, and salt. Using a pastry blender or two knives
   scissor-fashion, cut in the butter until the mixture resembles coarse
   meal. Add the milk and stir gently until the dough holds together.
3. Turn the dough out onto a floured surface and divide it into four
   equal pieces. Form each piece into a ball and place them on the
   prepared baking sheet. Pat each down into a 3-inch circle. Bake for
   15 to 20 minutes, or until golden brown. Remove from the oven and
   cool on a wire rack for 5 to 7 minutes before serving warm or cooled.

BASIC
POPOVERS
makes 10 to 12 popovers

1 cup all-purpose flour
½ tsp. salt
2 large eggs

1 cup milk
1 tbsp. butter or margarine,
melted

1. Position the rack in the center of the oven and preheat to 425 degrees.
   Liberally grease a 12-cup muffin baking pan or 12 oven-proof custard
   cups. Place in the oven until needed.
2. In a small bowl, blend together the flour and salt. In a medium bowl,
   beat the eggs until foamy. Beat in the milk and butter. Add the dry
   ingredients all at one time and beat until smooth.
3. Spoon the batter into the hot cups, filling each about ¾ full.
   Bake for 15 minutes (do not open the oven door). Reduce the heat
   to 375 degrees and bake for an additional 20 to 25 minutes, or until
   the tops are firm to the touch and a deep golden brown.
4. Turn off the oven, remove the popovers from the oven and prick the
   side of each popover with a fork. Return the popovers to the oven
   for an additional 5 minutes. Remove the popovers from the baking
   cups (run a knife around the edges of cups if necessary) and serve hot.

CHEESY MORNING POPOVERS

makes 6 to 8 popovers

1⅓ cups all-purpose flour	4 large eggs
½ cup shredded Swiss cheese	⅔ cup milk
½ tsp. salt	⅔ cup water

1. Position the rack in the center of the oven and preheat to 425 degrees. Liberally grease a 12-cup muffin baking pan or 12 oven-proof custard cups. Place in the oven until needed.
2. In a small bowl, blend together the flour, cheese, and salt. In a medium bowl, beat the eggs until foamy. Beat in the milk and water. Add the dry ingredients all at one time and beat until smooth.
3. Spoon the batter into the hot cups, filling each about ¾ full. Bake for 15 minutes (do not open the oven door). Reduce the heat to 375 degrees and bake for an additional 20 to 25 minutes, or until the tops are firm to the touch and a deep golden brown.
4. Turn off the oven, remove the popovers from the oven and prick the side of each popover with a fork. Return the popovers to the oven for an additional 5 minutes. Remove the popovers from the baking cups (run a knife around the edges of cups if necessary) and serve hot.

NEW ENGLAND
FAMILY POPOVERS

makes 6 to 8 popovers

1 tbsp. butter or margarine	¼ tsp. ground allspice
2 pounds tart apples, peeled, cored and diced	1 cup milk
	2 large eggs, separated
3 tbsp. granulated sugar	1 cup all-purpose flour
1 tsp. vanilla extract	¼ tsp. salt

1. In a large oven-proof skillet set over medium heat, melt the butter. Add the apples and 2 tablespoons of the sugar. Cook, stirring frequently, for 15 to 20 minutes or until the apples are tender and most of the liquid has evaporated. Remove from the heat and stir in the vanilla extract and allspice. Set aside.
2. Position the rack in the center of the oven and preheat to 425 degrees. In a medium bowl, beat the remaining tablespoon of sugar, the milk, egg yolks, flour, and salt until smooth. In a small bowl, beat the egg whites until stiff but not dry. Fold the egg whites into the yolk mixture.
3. Spoon the batter over the top of the apples in the skillet. Bake for 20 minutes (do not open the oven door). Reduce the heat to 350 degrees. and bake for an additional 10 to 15 minutes, or until the top of the popover is firm to the touch and golden brown. Remove the skillet from the oven and cool it on a wire rack for 3 to 5 minutes before cutting into wedges and serving.

ALMOND
BREAD

makes 1 loaf

1¼ cups sifted
  all-purpose flour
1½ tsp. baking powder
¼ cup almond halves
⅛ tsp. salt
	⅓ cup granulated sugar
	4 large eggs
	2 tbsp. lemon juice
	2 tbsp. melted butter
	  or margarine

1. Position the rack in the center of the oven and preheat to 375 degrees. Lightly grease and flour an 8-inch square baking pan.
2. In a large bowl, blend together the flour, baking powder, almonds, and salt. In a medium bowl, beat the sugar and eggs until smooth before beating in the lemon juice and butter. Combine the two mixtures, blending until the dry ingredients are moistened.
3. Scrape the batter into the prepared baking pan and bake for 35 to 40 minutes, or until a cake tester or wooden toothpick inserted into the center of the bread comes out clean and the top is golden brown. Remove from the oven and cool in the pan on a wire rack for 5 to 10 minutes before cutting into squares and serving.

APPLE-AND-CHERRY
BREAD

makes 1 loaf

1½ cups whole-wheat flour
1 cup all-purpose flour
1 cup rolled oats
1 tbsp. baking powder
1½ tsp. ground cinnamon
2 medium apples, peeled,
  cored, and finely chopped
1 cup candied cherry halves
½ cup golden raisins

1 tsp. grated lemon
  or orange zest
4 large eggs
¾ cup milk
½ cup apple-flavored yogurt
¼ cup unsweetened frozen
  apple-juice concentrate,
  thawed

1. Position the rack in the center of the oven and preheat to 350 degrees.
   Lightly grease and flour a 9 ¼ by 5 ½ by 2¾-inch loaf pan.
2. In a large bowl, blend together the two flours, oats, baking powder,
   cinnamon, apples, cherries, raisins, and lemon zest. In a medium
   bowl, beat the eggs until foamy before beating in the milk, yogurt,
   and apple juice. Combine the two mixtures, blending until the dry
   ingredients are thoroughly moistened.
3. Scrape the batter into the prepared pan and bake for 55 to 60 minutes,
   or until a cake tester or wooden toothpick inserted into the center of
   the bread comes out clean and the top is golden brown. Remove the
   pan from the oven and cool on a wire rack for 5 to 10 minutes
   before removing the loaf from the pan.

APRICOT-DATE BREAD

makes 1 loaf

1 cup all-purpose flour
½ cup whole-wheat flour
½ cup granulated sugar
2 tsp. baking powder
¼ tsp. baking soda
1 tbsp. grated orange zest
½ cup finely chopped
  dried apricots
½ cup finely chopped
  pitted dates
½ tsp. salt
¾ cup milk or light cream,
  at room temperature
1 large egg
1 tbsp. melted butter
  or margarine

1. Position the rack in the center of oven and preheat to 375 degrees. Lightly grease and flour an 8½ by 4½ by 2½-inch loaf pan.
2. In a large bowl, blend together the two flours, sugar, baking powder, baking soda, orange zest, apricots, dates, and salt. In a small bowl, beat the milk, egg, and butter until smooth. Combine the two mixtures, blending until the dry ingredients are just moistened.
3. Scrape the batter into the prepared pan and bake for 40 to 45 minutes, or until a cake tester or wooden toothpick inserted into the center of the bread comes out clean and the top is golden brown. Remove from the oven and cool the pan on a wire rack for 5 to 10 minutes before removing the loaf from the pan.

AVOCADO BREAD

makes 1 loaf

2 cups all-purpose flour
1½ tsp. baking powder
¼ cup granulated sugar
1 large egg
¼ cup melted butter
    or margarine

1 cup milk, at room
    temperature
1 medium avocado, pureed
1 cup toasted slivered almonds
    for topping

1. Position the rack in the center of the oven and preheat to 350 degrees.
   Lightly grease and flour an 8½ by 4½ by 2½-inch loaf pan.
2. In a large bowl, blend together the flour, baking powder, and sugar.
   In a medium bowl, beat the egg until foamy before beating in the
   butter, milk, and avocado. Combine the two mixtures, blending until
   the dry ingredients are moistened.
3. Scrape the batter into the prepared pan and bake for 45 to 50 minutes,
   or until a cake tester or wooden toothpick inserted into the center
   of the bread comes out clean and the top is golden brown. Remove
   from the oven and cool the pan on a wire rack for 5 to 10 minutes
   before removing the loaf from the pan. Sprinkle top with almonds.

BACON-CORN BREAD

makes 1 loaf

8 oz. sliced bacon
2 cups all-purpose flour
1½ cups cornmeal
¼ cup granulated sugar
2 tbsp. baking powder

2 tsp. salt
2 large eggs
1¼ cups milk
¼ cup vegetable oil

1. In a large skillet, cook the bacon until crisp. Drain, reserving ½ cup of the drippings, and cool the bacon on paper towels. When cooled, crumble and set aside.
2. Position the rack in the center of the oven and preheat to 400 degrees. Lightly grease and flour a 9-inch square baking pan.
3. In a large bowl, blend together the flour, cornmeal, sugar, baking powder, and salt. In a medium bowl, beat the eggs until foamy before beating in the milk, oil, and ½ cup reserved drippings. Combine the two mixtures, blending until the dry ingredients are just moistened.
4. Scrape the batter into the prepared pan and sprinkle the crumbled bacon over the top. Bake for 20 to 25 minutes, or until a cake tester or wooden toothpick inserted into the center of the bread comes out clean and the top is golden brown. Remove from the oven and cool the pan on a wire rack for 5 to 10 minutes before cutting into squares and serving.

BANANA-BLUEBERRY BREAD

makes 1 loaf

1½ cups whole-wheat flour
½ cup all-purpose flour
½ cup rolled oats
2 tsp. baking powder
½ tsp. baking soda
½ cup fresh or frozen
  blueberries

2 large egg whites
¼ cup melted butter
  or margarine
1 cup mashed bananas
¾ cup frozen apple-juice
  concentrate, thawed

1. Position the rack in the center of the oven and preheat to 325 degrees.
   Lightly grease and flour an 8½ by 4½ by 2½-inch loaf pan.
2. In a large bowl, blend together the two flours, oats, baking powder,
   and baking soda. Stir in the blueberries. In a medium bowl, beat the
   egg whites until stiff but not dry. Stir in the butter, bananas, and
   apple juice. Combine the two mixtures, blending until the dry
   ingredients are moistened.
3. Scrape the batter into the prepared pan and bake for 50 to 55 minutes,
   or until a cake tester or wooden toothpick inserted into the center
   of the bread comes out clean and the top is golden brown. Remove
   from the oven and cool the pan on a wire rack for 5 to 10 minutes
   before removing the loaf from the pan.

BANANA BREAD

makes 1 loaf

1½ cups all-purpose flour
1 cup oat flour
½ cup granulated sugar
1 tsp. baking powder
1 tsp. baking soda
1 tsp. ground cinnamon
½ cup flaked coconut
½ tsp. salt

2 large eggs
3 medium bananas, mashed
¼ cup canola oil
1 (8 oz.) can crushed pineapple
  (do not drain)
¼ cup shredded coconut
  for topping

1. Position the rack in the center of the oven and preheat to 350 degrees. Lightly grease and flour an 8½ by 4½ by 2½-inch loaf pan.
2. In a large bowl, blend together the two flours, sugar, baking powder, baking soda, cinnamon, coconut, and salt. In a medium bowl, beat the eggs until foamy before beating in the bananas, oil, and pineapple with its juice. Combine the two mixtures, blending until the dry ingredients are moistened.
3. Scrape the batter into the prepared pan and sprinkle the shredded coconut over the top. Bake for 45 to 50 minutes, or until a cake tester or wooden toothpick inserted into the center of the bread comes out clean and the top is golden brown. Remove from the oven and cool the pan on a wire rack for 5 to 10 minutes before removing the loaf from the pan.

BIRDSEED BREAD

makes 1 loaf

2 cups all-purpose flour
1 cup granulated sugar
2 tsp. baking powder
¼ tsp. ground cardamom
¼ cup poppy seeds
1 tsp. grated lemon zest

2 large eggs
½ cup butter or margarine, melted
2 medium ripe bananas, mashed

1. Position the rack in the center of the oven and preheat to 350 degrees. Lightly grease and flour an 8½ by 4½ by 2½-inch loaf pan.
2. In a large bowl, blend together the flour, sugar, baking powder, cardamom, poppy seeds, and lemon zest. In a medium bowl, beat the eggs until foamy before beating in the butter and bananas. Combine the two mixtures, blending until the dry ingredients are thoroughly moistened.
3. Scrape the batter into the prepared pan and bake for 45 to 50 minutes, or until a cake tester or wooden toothpick inserted into the center of the bread comes out clean and the top is golden brown. Remove from the oven and cool the pan on a wire rack for 5 to 10 minutes before removing the loaf from the pan.

BOSTON BROWN
BREAD

makes 3 to 4 small loaves

1 cup all-purpose flour
1 cup graham flour
1 cup cornmeal
1½ tsp. baking soda

1 tsp. salt
¾ cup molasses
2 cups sour milk or
buttermilk, warmed

1. Position the rack in the center of the oven and preheat to 350 degrees. Lightly grease and flour four 5¾ by 3 by 2⅛-inch loaf pans.
2. In a large bowl, blend together the two flours, cornmeal, baking soda, and salt. In a medium bowl, blend the molasses and warmed sour milk until smooth. Combine the two mixtures, blending until the dry ingredients are just moistened.
3. Scrape the batter into the prepared baking pans and bake for 40 to 45 minutes, or until a cake tester or wooden toothpick inserted into the center of the bread comes out clean and the tops are golden brown. Remove from the oven and cool the pans on a wire rack for 5 to 10 minutes before removing the loaves from the pans.

BRAZIL NUT–APRICOT BREAD

makes 1 loaf

2 cups all-purpose flour
1 cup granulated sugar
1 tbsp. baking powder
¼ tsp. baking soda
1 cup finely chopped
 Brazil nuts
½ cup chopped dried apricots

¾ tsp. salt
1 large egg
2 tbsp. melted butter
 or margarine
¾ cup fresh-squeezed
 orange juice

1. Position the rack in the center of the oven and preheat to 350 degrees. Lightly grease and flour an 8½ by 4½ by 2½-inch loaf pan.
2. In a large bowl, blend together the flour, sugar, baking powder, baking soda, nuts, apricots, and salt. In a small bowl, beat the egg, butter, and orange juice until smooth. Combine the two mixtures, blending until the dry ingredients are just moistened.
3. Scrape the batter into the prepared pan and bake for 45 to 50 minutes, or until a cake tester or wooden toothpick inserted into the center of the bread comes out clean and the top is golden brown. Remove from the oven and cool the pan on a wire rack for 5 to 10 minutes before removing the loaf from the pan.

BUTTERSCOTCH HAZELNUT BREAD
makes 1 loaf

2 cups all-purpose flour
1 cup packed light-brown
  sugar
1 tsp. baking powder
½ tsp. baking soda
½ cup chopped hazelnuts

¼ tsp. salt
1½ tbsp. melted butter or
  margarine
1 cup buttermilk or sour milk
1 large egg

1. Position the rack in the center of the oven and preheat to 350 degrees. Lightly grease and flour a 9¼ by 5¼ by 2¾-inch loaf pan.
2. In a large bowl, blend together the flour, brown sugar, baking powder, baking soda, hazelnuts, and salt. In a medium bowl, beat the butter, buttermilk, and egg until smooth. Combine the two mixtures, blending until the dry ingredients are moistened.
3. Scrape the batter into the prepared pan and bake for 55 to 60 minutes, or until a cake tester or wooden toothpick inserted into the center of the bread comes out clean and the top is golden brown. Remove from the oven and cool the pan on a wire rack for 5 to 10 minutes before removing the loaf from the pan.

CARAWAY BEER BREAD

makes 1 loaf

2 cups whole-wheat flour
1 cup all-purpose flour
1 cup granulated sugar
4 tsp. baking powder
1 tsp. baking soda
3 tbsp. caraway seeds
1 tsp. salt

2 large eggs
½ cup packed
  light-brown sugar
1¼ cups beer,
  at room temperature
½ cup maple syrup,
  slightly warmed

1 Position the rack in the center of the oven and preheat to 350 degrees.
   Lightly grease and flour a 9¼ by 5¼ by 2¾-inch loaf pan.
2 In a large bowl, blend together the two flours, granulated sugar,
   baking powder, baking soda, seeds, and salt. In a small bowl, beat
   the eggs, brown sugar, beer, and maple syrup until smooth. Combine
   the two mixtures, blending until the dry ingredients are moistened.
3 Scrape the batter into the prepared pan and bake for 55 to 60 minutes,
   or until a cake tester or wooden toothpick inserted into the center
   of the bread comes out clean and the top is golden brown. Remove
   from the oven and cool the pan on a wire rack for 5 to 10 minutes
   before removing the loaf from the pan.

CARDAMOM-HONEY BREAD

makes 1 loaf

1 cup all-purpose flour
1 cup whole-wheat flour
2½ cups oat or wheat bran
2 tsp. baking powder
1 tsp. baking soda
1 tsp. ground cardamom
¼ tsp. salt

4 large eggs
½ cup warmed honey
½ cup canola oil
¼ tsp. vanilla extract
2 cups unsweetened
  applesauce

1. Position the rack in the center of the oven and preheat to 350 degrees.
   Lightly grease and flour a 9¼ by 5¼ by 2¾-inch loaf pan.
2. In a large bowl, blend together the two flours, bran, baking powder,
   baking soda, salt, and cardamom. In a medium bowl, beat the eggs
   until foamy before beating in the honey, oil, and vanilla extract.
   Stir in the applesauce. Combine the two mixtures, blending until
   the dry ingredients are moistened.
3. Scrape the batter into the prepared pan and bake for 55 to 60
   minutes, or until a cake tester or wooden toothpick inserted into the
   center of the bread comes out clean and the top is golden brown.
   Remove the pan from the oven and cool on a wire rack for 5 to 10
   minutes before removing the loaf from the pan.

CHEDDAR
SPOON BREAD

makes 1 loaf

4 large eggs, separated
2 cups milk
1 cup cornmeal
2 cups (8 oz.) sharp
  Cheddar cheese, grated

½ cup margarine
1 tsp. salt
Pinch ground cayenne

1. Position the rack in the center of the oven and preheat to 375 degrees.
   Lightly grease and flour a 2-quart casserole dish.
2. In a medium bowl, beat the egg whites until stiff but not dry. Set aside.
   In a medium saucepan set over medium heat, heat the milk until
   bubbles start to form around the edges. Add the cornmeal and cook,
   stirring constantly, until the mixture is very thick and smooth. Remove
   from the heat and quickly stir in the cheese, margarine, salt, and
   cayenne, stirring until smooth. Stir in egg yolks. Fold in the egg whites.
3. Pour the mixture into the prepared baking dish and bake for 35 to 40
   minutes, or until the top is golden brown. Remove the casserole from
   the oven and serve immediately.

CREAM CHEESE BREAD

makes 2 loaves

2 cups all-purpose flour
1¼ tsp. baking powder
1 tsp. salt
1 package (8-oz.) cream cheese, at room temperature

1 cup butter or margarine, at room temperature
1 cup granulated sugar
3 large eggs

1. Position the rack in the center of the oven and preheat to 350 degrees. Lightly grease and flour two 8½ by 4½ by 2½-inch loaf pans.
2. In a large bowl, blend together the flour, baking powder, and salt. In a medium bowl, beat the cheese, butter, and sugar together until smooth. Beat in the eggs, one at a time, beating vigorously after each addition. Combine the two mixtures, blending until the dry ingredients are well moistened.
3. Scrape the batter into the prepared pans and bake for 45 to 50 minutes, or until a cake tester or wooden toothpick inserted into the center of the bread comes out clean and the tops are golden brown. Remove from the oven and cool the pans on a wire rack for 5 to 10 minutes before removing the loaves from the pans.

ENRICHED PRUNE BREAD

makes 1 loaf

1 package (12 oz.) pitted prunes, coarsely chopped
1 cup freshly squeezed orange juice
⅔ cup granulated sugar
¼ cup butter or margarine, at room temperature
⅓ cup Triple Sec liqueur
1 tsp. lemon or orange extract

1½ cups all-purpose flour
½ cup whole-wheat flour
1 tsp. baking powder
1 tsp. baking soda
¾ tsp. ground cinnamon
¼ tsp. ground cloves
Coarsely grated orange zest for topping

1. Position the rack in the center of the oven and preheat to 350 degrees. Lightly grease and flour an 8½ by 4½ by 2½-inch loaf pan.

2. In a medium saucepan, combine the prunes, orange juice, sugar, and butter and set over medium heat. Cook until bubbles form around the edges of the pan. Remove from the heat and stir in the Triple Sec and flavored extract. Set aside to cool.

3. In a large bowl, blend together the two flours, baking powder, baking soda, cinnamon, and cloves. Combine the dry ingredients with the prune mixture, blending until the dry ingredients are moistened.

4. Scrape the batter into the prepared pan and sprinkle the orange zest over the top. Bake for 45 to 50 minutes, or until a cake tester or wooden toothpick inserted into the center of the bread comes out clean and the top is golden brown. Remove from the oven and cool the pan on a wire rack for 5 to 10 minutes before removing the loaf from the pan.

GRAPE NUT
APRICOT BREAD

makes 1 loaf

2 cups hot scalded milk
1 cup Grape Nuts® cereal
1 cup finely chopped dried
  apricots
3 cups all-purpose flour
½ cup granulated sugar

4 tsp. baking powder
1½ tsp. salt
1 large egg
3 tbsp. melted butter
  or margarine

1. Position the rack in the center of the oven and preheat to 350 degrees.
   Lightly grease and flour a 9¼ by 5¼ by 2¾-inch loaf pan.
2. In a small bowl, combine the milk, cereal, and apricots. Set aside
   to cool.
3. In a large bowl, blend together the flour, sugar, baking powder,
   and salt. In a medium bowl, beat the egg until foamy before beating
   in the butter. Stir in the cooled cereal mixture. Combine the wet and dry
   mixtures, blending until the dry ingredients are thoroughly moistened.
4. Scrape the batter into the prepared pan and bake for 55 to 60
   minutes, or until a cake tester or wooden toothpick inserted into the
   center of the bread comes out clean and the top is golden brown.
   Remove from the oven and cool the pan on a wire rack for 5 to 10
   minutes before removing the loaf from the pan.

HERBED TOMATO BREAD

makes 1 loaf

3 cups all-purpose flour
2½ tsp. baking powder
½ tsp. baking soda
2 tbsp. snipped
  fresh tarragon
1 tbsp. snipped fresh parsley
1 tbsp. granulated sugar
1 cup finely grated
  Cheddar cheese
½ tsp. salt

2 large eggs
1 cup milk
¼ cup canola oil
2 tbsp. tomato paste
1 small yellow onion,
  finely chopped
1 tsp. ketchup
½ cup grated Provolone cheese
  for topping

1. Position the rack in the center of the oven and preheat to 350 degrees. Lightly grease and flour a 9¼ by 5¼ by 2¾-inch loaf pan.

2. In a large bowl, blend together the flour, baking powder, baking soda, tarragon, parsley, sugar, cheese, and salt. In a medium bowl, beat the eggs until foamy before beating in the milk, oil, tomato paste, onion, and ketchup. Combine the two mixtures, blending until the dry ingredients are moistened.

3. Scrape the batter into the prepared pan and sprinkle the Provolone over the top. Bake for 55 to 60 minutes, or until a cake tester or wooden toothpick inserted into the center of the bread comes out clean and the top is golden brown. Remove from the oven and cool the pan on a wire rack for 5 to 10 minutes before removing the loaf from the pan.

ITALIAN-STYLE
PROSCIUTTO BREAD

makes 1 loaf

2½ cups all-purpose flour
1¾ tsp. baking powder
½ tsp. baking soda
5 slices Parma ham
  (Prosciutto), chopped
⅓ cup chopped sun-dried
  tomatoes
2 tbsp. snipped
  fresh basil

1½ tsp. garlic powder
1 large egg
½ cup light olive oil
1¼ cups buttermilk
  or sour milk
Freshly ground black pepper
  to taste
Shredded Provolone cheese
  for topping

1. Position the rack in the center of the oven and preheat to 350 degrees.
   Lightly grease and flour a 9-inch square baking pan.
2. In a large bowl, blend together the flour, baking powder, baking
   soda, ham, tomatoes, basil, and garlic powder. In a medium bowl,
   beat the egg, oil, and buttermilk until smooth. Combine the two
   mixtures, blending until the dry ingredients are moistened.
3. Scrape the batter into the prepared pan and sprinkle with Provolone
   cheese. Bake for 40 to 45 minutes, or until a cake tester or wooden
   toothpick inserted into the center of the bread comes out clean and the
   top is golden brown. Remove from the oven and cool in the pan on a
   wire rack for 5 to 10 minutes before removing the loaf from the pan.

ORANGE MARMALADE
NUT BREAD

makes 1 loaf

2 cups all-purpose flour
¾ cup graham flour
2 tsp. baking powder
½ tsp. baking soda
½ cup chopped walnuts
½ tsp. salt
½ cup butter or margarine,
  at room temperature

½ cup packed light-brown sugar
2 large eggs
1 (10 oz.) jar orange
  marmalade
½ cup freshly squeezed
  orange juice

1. Position the rack in the center of the oven and preheat to 350 degrees. Lightly grease and flour an 8½ by 4½ by 2½-inch loaf pan.
2. In a large bowl, blend together the two flours, baking powder, baking soda, walnuts, and salt. In a medium bowl, beat the butter and brown sugar until smooth before beating in the eggs, one at a time, beating vigorously after each addition. Beat in the marmalade and juice. Combine the two mixtures, blending until the dry ingredients are moistened.
3. Scrape the batter into the prepared pan and bake for 55 to 60 minutes, or until a cake tester or wooden toothpick inserted into the center of the bread comes out clean and the top is golden brown. Remove from the oven and cool the pan on a wire rack for 5 to 10 minutes before removing the loaf from the pan.

PEANUT BUTTER-BACON BREAD

makes 1 loaf

2 cups all-purpose flour
1 cup granulated sugar
1 tbsp. baking powder
1 cup crumbled
  crisply cooked bacon, plus
  more for topping the bread
1 cup coarsely chopped
  unsalted peanuts

½ tsp. salt
1 large egg
1 tbsp. melted butter
  or margarine
1 cup milk
1 cup peanut butter
Honey for brushing

1. Position the rack in the center of the oven and preheat to 350 degrees. Lightly grease and flour an 8½ by 4½ by 2½-inch loaf pan.
2. In a large bowl, blend together the flour, sugar, baking powder, one cup crumbled bacon, peanuts, and salt. In a medium bowl, beat the egg until foamy before beating in the butter, milk, and peanut butter. Combine the two mixtures, blending until the dry ingredients are moistened.
3. Scrape the batter into the prepared pan and bake for 45 to 50 minutes, or until a cake tester or wooden toothpick inserted into the center of the bread comes out clean and the top is golden brown. Remove from the oven and cool the pan on a wire rack for 5 to 10 minutes before removing the loaf from the pan. Brush the loaf with honey and sprinkle with additional crumbled bacon.

PINEAPPLE-NUT BREAD

makes 1 loaf

2 cups all-purpose flour
2 tsp. baking powder
¼ tsp. baking soda
2 tbsp. granulated sugar
½ tsp. ground cardamom
¾ cup chopped chestnuts
  or black walnuts
½ cup finely chopped
  seedless raisins

2 large eggs
¾ cup packed dark-brown sugar
3 tbsp. melted butter
  or margarine
1 (8 oz.) can crushed
  pineapple, undrained

1. Position the rack in the center of the oven and preheat to 350 degrees. Lightly grease and flour an 8½ by 4½ by 2½-inch loaf pan.
2. In a large bowl, blend together the flour, baking powder, baking soda, granulated sugar, cardamom, chestnuts, and raisins. In a medium bowl, beat the eggs until foamy before beating in the brown sugar and butter. Stir in the pineapple. Combine the two mixtures, blending until the dry ingredients are thoroughly moistened.
3. Scrape the batter into the prepared pan and bake for 55 to 60 minutes, or until a cake tester or wooden toothpick inserted into the center of the bread comes out clean and the top is golden brown. Remove from the oven and cool the pan on a wire rack for 5 to 10 minutes before removing the loaf from the pan.

PLANTATION
HERB BREAD

makes 1 loaf

2 cups all-purpose flour
1 tbsp. baking powder
1 cup cooked brown
  or wild rice
¼ tsp. dried crushed thyme
½ tsp. dried crushed basil
¼ tsp. dried crushed parsley

¼ cup grated Parmesan
  or Romano cheese
2 large eggs
1 cup milk
3 tbsp. melted butter
  or margarine

1. Position the rack in the center of the oven and preheat to 350 degrees.
   Lightly grease and flour a 9¼ by 5¼ by 2¾-inch loaf pan.
2. In a large bowl, blend together the flour, baking powder, rice, herbs,
   and cheese. In a medium bowl, beat the eggs until foamy before
   beating in the milk and butter. Combine the two mixtures, blending
   until the dry ingredients are well moistened.
3. Scrape the batter into the prepared pan and bake for 55 to 60
   minutes, or until a cake tester or wooden toothpick inserted into the
   center of the bread comes out clean and the top is golden brown.
   Remove from the oven and cool the pan on a wire rack for 5 to 10
   minutes before removing the loaf from the pan.

QUICK FRUIT BREAD

makes 1 loaf

1 cup all-purpose flour
1 cup whole-wheat flour
½ cup soy flour
½ cup oat bran
1 tsp. baking soda
1 cup chopped nuts (optional)
½ tsp. salt
¼ cup butter or margarine,
   at room temperature

½ cup granulated sugar
1 large egg
¼ cup fresh juice or
   berry-flavored liqueur
1 cup fruit pulp
1 cup sour milk or buttermilk

1. Position the rack in the center of the oven and preheat to 350 degrees.
   Lightly grease and flour a 9¼ by 5¼ by 2¾-inch loaf pan.
2. In a large bowl, blend together the three flours, oat bran, baking
   soda, nuts, and salt. In a medium bowl, beat the butter and sugar
   until light and fluffy. Beat in the egg, juice, pulp, and sour milk.
   Combine the two mixtures, blending until the dry ingredients are
   well moistened.
3. Scrape the batter into the prepared pan and bake for 55 to 60 minutes,
   or until a cake tester or wooden toothpick inserted into the center
   of the bread comes out clean and the top is golden brown. Remove
   from the oven and cool the pan on a wire rack for 5 to 10 minutes
   before removing the loaf from the pan.

TANGERINE TEA BREAD

makes 1 loaf

1½ cups all-purpose flour
½ cup graham flour
2½ tsp. baking powder
¼ tsp. baking soda
3 tbsp. finely minced
   tangerine peel
½ cup chopped pecans
   or macadamia nuts

1 tsp. salt
1 large egg
½ cup freshly squeezed
   tangerine juice
½ cup milk or light cream
¼ cup melted butter
   or margarine

1. Position the rack in the center of the oven and preheat to 350 degrees. Lightly grease and flour an 8½ by 4½ by 2½-inch loaf pan.
2. In a large bowl, blend together the two flours, baking powder, baking soda, peel, pecans, and salt. In a small bowl, beat the egg until foamy before beating in the juice, milk, and butter. Combine the two mixtures, blending until the dry ingredients are moistened.
3. Scrape the batter into the prepared pan and bake for 55 to 60 minutes, or until a cake tester or wooden toothpick inserted into the center of the bread comes out clean and the top is golden brown. Remove from the oven and cool the pan on a wire rack for 5 to 10 minutes before removing the loaf from the pan.

ZUCCHINI BREAD

makes 1 loaf

2½ cups all-purpose flour
1 tsp. baking powder
1 tsp. baking soda
2 tsp. ground cinnamon
1 cup finely chopped
   seedless raisins
½ tsp. salt

2 large eggs
¾ cup melted margarine
   or butter
1 tsp. almond extract
1½ cups warm honey
2 cups grated zucchini

1. Position the rack in the center of the oven and preheat to 350 degrees.
   Lightly grease and flour a 9¼ by 5¼ by 2¾-inch loaf pan.
2. In a large bowl, blend together the flour, baking powder, baking
   soda, cinnamon, raisins, and salt. In a medium bowl, beat the eggs
   until foamy before beating in the margarine, almond extract, and
   honey. Stir in the zucchini. Combine the two mixtures, blending until
   the dry ingredients are well moistened.
3. Scrape the batter into the prepared pan and bake for 55 to 60 minutes,
   or until a cake tester or wooden toothpick inserted into the center
   of the bread comes out clean and the top is golden brown. Remove
   from the oven and cool the pan on a wire rack for 5 to 10 minutes
   before removing the loaf from the pan.

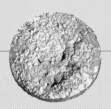

BLACKBERRY-LEMON COFFEE CAKE

makes 6 to 8 servings

¾ cup crushed crisped
  rice cereal
1½ cups all-purpose flour
¾ cup granulated sugar
½ cup butter or margarine,
  at room temperature
½ tsp. baking powder

½ tsp. baking soda
¼ tsp. salt
1 large egg
¾ cup buttermilk or sour milk
1 tsp. grated lemon zest
½ cup blackberry preserves

1. Position the rack in the center of the oven and preheat to 350 degrees. Lightly grease a 9-inch square or round baking pan.
2. In a large bowl, blend together the cereal, flour, and sugar. Using a pastry cutter or two knives scissor-fashion, cut in the margarine until the mixture resembles coarse meal. Reserve ½ cup of this mixture for topping. To the remainder, blend in the baking powder, baking soda, and salt. In a medium bowl, beat the egg until foamy before beating in the buttermilk and lemon zest. Combine the two mixtures, blending until the dry ingredients are moistened.
3. Spoon ⅔ of the batter into the prepared pan. Gently spread the blackberry preserves over the top. Dot the remaining batter over the top of the preserves. Sprinkle the reserved crumble mix over the top.
4. Bake for 35 to 40 minutes, or until a cake tester or wooden toothpick inserted near the edge of the cake (not into the preserves) comes out clean. Remove the pan from the oven and cool on a wire rack for 5 to 7 minutes. Serve warm.

CHOCOLATE COFFEE CAKE

makes 10 to 12 servings

½ cup finely ground almonds
2 ½ cups all-purpose flour
2 tsp. baking powder
1 tsp. baking soda
¼ tsp. salt
½ cup Dutch-processed
  cocoa powder
1½ cups dried apricots,
  finely diced

1 cup vegetable shortening
1 package (8 oz.) cream cheese,
  at room temperature
2¼ cups granulated sugar
5 large eggs
1½ tsp. Amaretto liqueur

1. Position the rack in the center of the oven and preheat to 350 degrees. Grease and flour a 10-inch Bundt pan. Press ¼ cup of the almonds up the outer sides of the pan.
2. In a large bowl, blend together the remaining almonds, flour, baking powder, baking soda, salt, cocoa powder, and diced apricots. In a medium bowl, beat shortening, cream cheese, and sugar until smooth. Beat in the eggs one at a time, beating vigorously after each addition. Beat in the Amaretto. Combine the two mixtures, blending until the dry ingredients are just moistened.
3. Carefully spoon the batter into the prepared baking pan. Bake for 45 to 50 minutes, or until a cake tester or wooden toothpick inserted into the center of the cake comes out clean. Remove the pan from the oven and cool on a wire rack for 5 to 7 minutes before inverting onto a wire rack to cool completely. Serve warm.

CINNAMON
COFFEE CAKE
makes 8 to 10 servings

½ cup firmly packed
  brown sugar
½ cup finely chopped walnuts
2 tbsp. all-purpose flour
2 tsp. ground cinnamon
2 tbsp. canola oil
1½ cups all-purpose flour

½ cup granulated sugar
2½ tsp. baking powder
½ tsp. salt
1 large egg white
¼ cup canola oil
¾ cup milk

1. Position the rack in the center of the oven and preheat to 375 degrees.
   Lightly grease and flour the bottom of an 8-inch square or round
   baking pan.
2. To make the topping, in a small bowl, combine the brown sugar,
   walnuts, flour, cinnamon, and oil and mix until crumbly. Set aside.
3. To make the batter, in a large bowl, blend together the flour, sugar,
   baking powder, and salt. In a medium bowl, beat the egg white until
   foamy before beating in the oil and milk. Combine the two mixtures,
   blending until the dry ingredients are moistened.
4. Spoon half of the batter into the prepared baking pan and top the
   batter with half of the topping. Spoon the remaining batter into the
   pan and top with the remaining topping. Bake for 30 to 35 minutes,
   or until a cake tester or wooden toothpick inserted into the center
   of the cake comes out clean. Remove the pan from the oven and
   cool on a wire rack for 5 to 7 minutes. Serve warm or cooled.

FAT-FREE APPLE COFFEE CAKE

makes 8 to 10 servings

1 cup all-purpose flour
1½ tsp. baking powder
¾ cup granulated sugar
½ tsp. salt
2 large egg whites
⅓ cup skim milk

⅓ cup light or dark corn syrup
2 apples, peeled, cored,
   and halved
2 tbsp. cinnamon sugar
   for sprinkling

1. Position the rack in the center of the oven and preheat to 350 degrees.
   Lightly grease and flour the bottom of a 9-inch square or round
   baking pan.
2. In a large bowl, blend together the flour, baking powder, sugar,
   and salt. In a medium bowl, beat the egg whites stiff but not dry
   before beating in the milk and corn syrup. Combine the two mixtures,
   blending until the dry ingredients are moistened. Spoon the batter
   into the prepared pan, arrange the apples over the top, and sprinkle
   with cinnamon sugar.
3. Bake for 45 to 50 minutes, or until a cake tester or wooden toothpick
   inserted into the center of the cake comes out clean. Remove the pan
   from the oven and cool on a wire rack for 5 to 7 minutes. Serve warm.

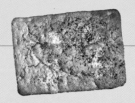

PECAN SOUR CREAM
COFFEE CAKE

makes 11 to 12 servings

¾ cup firmly packed
  brown sugar
1 tbsp. all-purpose flour
1 tsp. ground cinnamon
2 tbsp. butter or margarine,
  at room temperature
1 cup chopped pecans
½ cup butter or margarine

1 cup granulated sugar
3 large eggs
1 cup sour cream
2 cups all-purpose flour
1 tsp. baking powder
1 tsp. baking soda
½ cup raisins
¼ tsp. salt

1. Position the rack in the center of the oven and preheat to 350 degrees.
   Lightly grease and flour the bottom of a 13 by 9-inch baking pan.

2. To make the topping, in a small bowl, combine the brown sugar, flour,
   and cinnamon. Cut in the butter until mixture is crumbly. Set aside.

3. To make the batter, in a medium bowl, beat the butter and sugar until
   light and fluffy. Add the eggs, one at a time, beating vigorously after
   each addition. Add the sour cream. In a large bowl, blend together
   the flour, the baking powder, baking soda, raisins, and salt. Combine
   the two mixtures, blending until the dry ingredients are moistened.

4. Spoon the batter into the prepared pan and sprinkle the topping over
   the batter. Bake for 28 to 30 minutes, or until a cake tester or
   wooden toothpick inserted into the center of the cake comes out
   clean. Remove the pan from the oven and cool on a wire rack for 5
   to 7 minutes. Serve warm.